Flower Petals of
MEMORIES

Authentic Self Series

Selaih K. Lewis-Nguessan

Artist: Stephen Adams

AuthorHouse™
1663 Liberty Drive
Bloomington, IN 47403
www.authorhouse.com
Phone: 1 (800) 839-8640

Published by AuthorHouse 05/21/2015

ISBN: 978-1-5049-0353-0 (sc)
ISBN: 978-1-5049-1406-2 (hc)
ISBN: 978-1-5049-0354-7 (e)

Library of Congress Control Number 2015904793

Print information available on the last page.

Any people depicted in stock imagery provided by Thinkstock are models,
and such images are being used for illustrative purposes only.
Certain stock imagery © Thinkstock.

This book is printed on acid-free paper.

authorHOUSE®

To those who have endured many challenges in life, but persevere to seek enlightenment to evolve and live fearlessly with joy and passion.

Stay well and cherished!

This book is written in loving memory of the women that encouraged me to soar, starting with my maternal great-grandmother Corine Askew (Dee), maternal grandmother Lafalene Stewart and paternal grandmother Mable Lee Turner.

****

I also wish to thank the following people:

My mother, Gwendolyn Woodson, who inspired my voice, creativity, and humanitarianism.

My father, Tommy Ti El, my biggest fan and mentor; who inspired my delightful wit, confidence, and tenacity.

My sisters, Tracey Woodson-Martin and Cherise Olmo; the commitment and strength of our sisterhood is a powerful force to be reckoned with priceless and unshakable!

My cherished childhood friend, Arnesa Williams-Joplin, whose honesty and unconditional friendship keeps me grounded.

I thank you all for the invaluable lessons you gave me.

Contents

'Ode To My Great-Grandmother 45

A Feeling Comes 7

A Humble Prayer 33

A Ray Of Golden Light 49

A Reflective Sun 9

Acknowledgment 5

Feeling You 11

Go On And Do Your Thing 13

He Gives Me Victory 15

I Cried A River 17

I Need To Leave You Alone 19

I Should've 32

I'll Only Come 25

Longing 29

Loveland 31

My Intended, So Sweet...35

My Love Comes...37

No Lie...43

See Me..53

Sister To Sister..55

Sitting Here..57

Solitude Groove 41

Time To Make A Change..61

Transform 65

Trying To Find My Way...69

What If I Flipped On You? 77

You Only Had To Say...73

You Put The Color Back In My Life 75

Acknowledgment

To Pelagie Kouadio: Thank you for listening to me and helping me at this stage in my life. Your insistence that I share my gifts to inspire others was just the push that I needed.

To my sugar bears, JB and Shale: Thank you for your unconditional love and for adding renewed purpose to my life. My love for you is infinite as the universe!

To my anchor of support, my husband, Kouassi: Thank you for sharing this life with me and for accepting me as the woman I've grown to be. You still look at me with the same adoration as you did on the day we met many years ago. That alone is more than any woman could ask for in a partner. I say, "I do," again!

A Feeling Comes

A feeling comes over me like the strike from a bite that stings the senses. The venom is forever relentless as my body attempts to adjust during the day and throughout the night. It's the quake in the soul as once I was told. To conquer, it takes the patience of the sloth to attract the moth with light from one single pill. I try to refrain, but the symptoms are contracting, impacting even still.

A smile, a straight face, a quick yes or no is all I have to answer. I'm not here or there; only within do I spin. I care not for the lighthearted banter. I'm never one to gloat, but when he's around, I'm flowery and mellow like mulberry wine from the swirling vine, causing giddiness as we stand in unison to christen the boat. No need for the remote. We enjoy the manual feel.

I like red, orange, green, and yellow. He's an operation of meditation and with fine sutures, I stitch peaceful pathways to his Zen. I'm within. Staying close, and closer I stay, for he's my magnet. I've got to have it long, strong, and vibrant with might. Indeed a magnificent fellow, never one to flinch from the pinch of this life. Yes, I said it. That's right. He's an undeniable thrill.

He carries the flame, but who am I to blame? With no chagrin, he's a ten, and that's all that matters. His meekness is my all-encompassing weakness. I reach, he peaks, and we flutter from the rumble. The antidote exists within the unspoken code: a smile, a sway, a hold to mold. Fingertips and lips caressing the blessing, for I am his and truly humbled.

A feeling comes over me like the strike from a bite that stings the senses. The venom is forever relentless; it debilitates. We search high and low for the solution to this pollution. Clear the line and tap the vein; induce the drip, and together we sip, filling up just enough. For in my ocean, there's a priceless potion filled with treasure, but only for his unyielding pleasure, I decree. We're caught up in the revelry as we glide on love, commitment, and truth, the beat of our resounding devotion. This love overcomes, and for this, a feeling comes.

A Reflective Sun

I sat down on a bench the other day to pass the time. In muted silence, I watched the cars and people pass to and fro. They were all in a rush, with no time to spare one dime. This vision put me in a haze but even more like a reflective daze. And all of a sudden, thoughts of you came to me like whispers on the September breeze. The colors of you, creating a familiar echo.

On a good day, I'm steady and strong. I take each task in stride, stay focused, and try not to allow the submission. And even though it was so long ago, the ending still perplexes my sensitive ego. I only wanted to hold out for one last evening intermission. It was inevitable that it had to cease. We both knew this. But, be honest: Did we ever experience a true release?

It's the release that mere words could not describe. The eyes alone spoke of the intention, like highway billboards constantly flashing the permission. The sights and sounds, slowly lulling us into an intoxicating trance. Only our bodies, moving in mutual harmony, knew the steps to this ritualistic and ancient dance.

I tried to put rhyme to reason—rounded to the nearest ten and even carried the one. It never seemed to balance out. But it was well worth the experience and it created such an exciting memory. It was what I'd call quite an adventure. Yes, we discovered some fun!

I sat down on a bench the other day to pass the time. In muted silence, I watched the cars and people pass to and fro. They were all in a rush, with no time to spare one dime. Yes, I remember that September. You were my ease on the warm September breeze, a beacon of light to comfort and protect me—a reflective sun.

Feeling You

I'm feeling you all over me. Come to me.

Needing you all over me. Undo me.

If I told you that I wanted to rearrange and make a new frame with you, would you hold that against me, darling?

And you know that I'd do: whatever it takes to be in your space, spend the rest of my life with you. Breathe into me.

Open your eyes and realize. You're amazing, stimulating, and you got me saying,

"I feel for you." And, darling, you know I do. With your eyes caressing me.

This love is so complete. It's all I need, for me.

I'm feeling you; feeling you—all over, over me.

Hand in hand, we'll find a better way. I'll make a new chain with you, up and over, through and through.

It's so amazing. There's no limit, no higher rate with you. Charge me up—no limit.

Open your eyes and realize. I'm motivated, elevated, and you got me saying,

"I feel for you." And, darling, you know I do. We're forever together now,

because, darling, I do thee! You're a part of me, for me.

I'm feeling you; feeling you—all over, over me.

Go On And Do Your Thing

Go on and do your thing. I'm not mad at you. May this life continue to bless you. Sing your song, loud and strong. You deserve to be happy, self-fulfilled and to live long. Further your tribe, wife, children, and success; be blessed, and continue to thrive. Continue to be true, and don't change, but be rearranged to improve as we all endeavor to strive.

Do it with palms up and open to show no secrets, no shade. Be a straight-up man. Be free to show your love, passionately; for once, just give in. Love is a beautiful thing, like the birds and bees, as the lover sings.

Take your chance; don't dilly or dally. Many people don't get the opportunity to have such a true romance. Don't look back; move into your future with hope, aspiration, and tact. Be resolved in what you stand for. From a child running wild to a man with a plan, stay focused and evolve.

Go on and give with good intention, not waiting for a return. By this code of ethics, we aim to live and learn. Fly high to achieve your goals and receive full commission. Keep moving forward, and never give up. There's no need for anyone's permission.

Go on and do your thing. I'm not mad at you. Go on, do it!

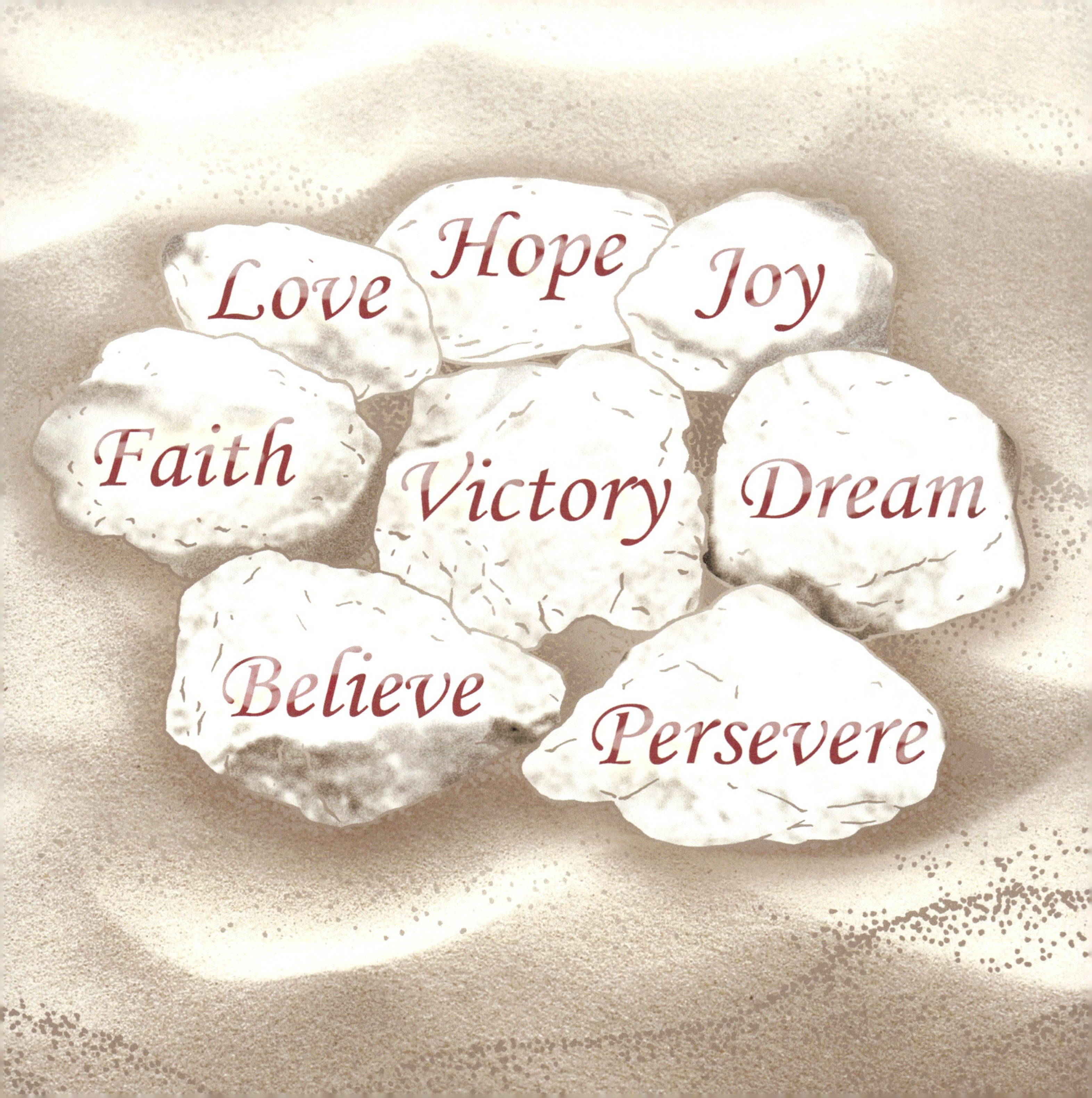
Love
Hope
Joy
Faith
Victory
Dream
Believe
Persevere

He Gives Me Victory

When I look back upon my life, I see all the blessings He's given me. I've journeyed through darkness, woes, and strife, but still He sheltered me.

Through times of struggle, He made a way far greater than my eyes could see. Thank you Father, for your mercy and for showing me like Jesus, we should strive to be.

He gives me victory! He gives me victory!

No turning back. I'm on the path—to the road that leads to Thee.

He gives me victory! He gives me victory!

No turning back. I'll remain steadfast on the road that leads to Thee

Living in this life, keep the Lord on your side. He's my protector, my joy, and pride. He's the alpha and omega. He's the day and night; my master and guiding light.

Though friends may come and loved ones go, my redeemer you'll always be. And when the end of my time draws near and my body is worn and weak. I will praise your name. I will remain your servant, faithfully.

He gives me victory! Oh, He gives me victory!

No turning back. It's a proven fact. I'm on the road that leads to Thee

He gives me victory! He gives me victory!

No turning back. I'm on the path to the road that leads to Thee. Amen!

I Cried A River

I cried a river last night.

I couldn't help it. All the signs told me that something wasn't right. This river came in the form of torrential aches, strong pains, and huge moans. It was hard to control, and it almost took my last breath. I reached out for an anchor of reassurance, but absolutely nothing was left. I cried a river until the source ran dry, and then I sat on the edge of the bank, trying to compose myself before giving in to this foreboding good-bye.

I cried a river until the water ran cold. I felt out of it and a bit displaced. You could've bought me for twenty-five cents. Down the river, I was sold. It shook me and took me. I was mercilessly spent. Together, we cried a river.

I cried a river until the water ran under. I knew it was a foolish mission, but it was worth it—such a sweet blunder. They call it the purge, but as much as I try to free myself, I still show the symptoms of that undeniable urge.

I cried a river until it ran over. I can still remember how we sat close to each other, no words needing to be spoken, but communicating through silent emotion. And in the air was the faint scent of honeysuckle and fresh-cut clover.

I cried a river until it ran high, forever missing the times we joined together and effortlessly touched that sky. I cried for the beauty of it all—the laughter, joy and the inevitable fall.

It was time to move on to higher ground, greener pastures. But through the ebb and flow, I realized that love is the true keeper. It is a lifeline. This truth, I will always know.

I cried a river last night.

It served as an end to this quest. Time to redirect my sails and face a new wind. But you will always be a treasured friend, and our memories are forever ingrained deep within my chest.

I cried a river until the river ran blue. I remembered your smile and that endearing guile and like the river, I cried too.

I Need To Leave You Alone

I need to leave you alone and cease this aimless roam over you and through you, inside and out. But I saw you the other day, and I swear that your vibe kept me alive. In me, through me, no doubt: Love always finds a way.

I need to stop this pacing and racing—foolish me. Can you believe that at times, I've even thought of us as one big ol' happy family? But I remember when your fingertips softly caressed my skin in the middle of the night. Was it the moon or the stars above us? I don't know, nor do I care. But what I do know is that it felt good, so right.

When we are apart, you can't imagine the shift it creates within my spirit. It sounds silly, huh? But the feelings are mutual and I know you feel it. When you smile at me with your eyes, the electricity is so unnerving. I stand firm to receive it all; absolutely no swerving.

Maybe it's time to stop chasing a lost dream, all those moments from that elusive past, and cherish our brief time together in the present and hope that it will endure and somehow last. But when you speak to me, I slowly become submerged in your vortex of gentleness and playful seduction. I'm strong, but your quiet force is powerful, and it causes such an overflow of eruption.

This obsession is an unpredictable possession, and I'm still asking, how could this be? I must admit that I enjoy how you warm my soul and make it smile like the radiant sun for all to see. But you still don't comprehend the depth of how you inspire me.

I need to leave you alone because I see your wants and feel your desires. But don't get it twisted. I'm definitely optimistic. My wish has always been for you to succeed, fly higher, and be committed.

This life is merely like the span of a hand: unpredictable, with highs and lows. I'm much older and wiser, and I enjoy being free. Considering our history together, I don't hold back with you. I'm sure you've grown to understand this, by now, about me. I acquiesce and hold no regrets for how things turned out to be. I adore the memories and want to thank you kindly for sharing a portion of this fascinating life with yours truly. Yes, forever in your flower petals of memory: blossoms of me.

I need to leave you alone and give it a rest. But I can't help it that I think you're a beautiful soul. I'm attracted to your essence, and going our separate ways is for the best. But when it's all said and done and we've reached that age of twilight, with hairs all grayed. Nothing else will matter but to reflect upon the faded shadows of the treasured memories we created. You were the one who helped renew and ease me through my transition from being a wilted flower with an unrelenting thirst that needed to be soothed and showered with your waters to reach full blossom, like a rebirth. And after all these years, through the pages of my successes, joys, and tears, now I truly understand my undeniable self-worth. So, cheers! You have been such an unforgettable dear. I thank you. I release you.

I Should've

I should've loved you in a time and place.

I should've loved you forever.

I should've loved you and erased the trace, through space and time that's the measure.

> When the storms come, falling on me, all I need is your love. Wrap your
>
> loving arms around me. I'll never break from your love.
>
> I should've when the storms came falling on me.
>
> I should've when the world was strong against me.
>
> All I need is your love. All I want is your touch.

I never wanted to be replaced, but my foolish pride made you sever.

Please forgive me. Open up your heart. I'm not the same. I'll never leave you ever.

I give to you my love, my heart, and my soul. Come back to me. You're my loving treasure.

> When the storms come falling on me, all I need is your love. Wrap your
>
> loving arms around me. I'll never break from your love.
>
> I should've when the storms came falling on me.
>
> I should've when the world was strong against me.
>
> All I need is your love. All I want is your touch.

I'll Only Come

I'll only come if you promise to let me in through a window of your heart. And then we'll rise to greet one another on a feverish beat of unrestrained emotion as you slowly pull back the shades to let the moonlight shine through. This force compels us to pause to catch a shaky breath and bask in the glow of an experience that was so long overdue. Do you feel me now? Good, because I most certainly do you.

Promise to light three candles: one of vanilla, another of sandalwood, and the last of patchouli. These will symbolize the innocence of youthful days that were, the desire that is, and the memories that will forever remain.

Promise to be yourself, unpretentious and true. For once, stake claim to your feelings. Whisper your melodic serenade as we float along the misty banks, cloaked in a rhapsody of our own home-grown magic. We lose track of time as we create our fertile oasis of refuge along the shoreline of sweet serenity and experience the ebb and flow of unrelenting passion. My aura radiates around you like musical notes on wings of caresses to torment your senses and keep you forever enchanted.

I'll only come if you promise to let me run my fingers through your glorious mane unabashedly—to feel its texture and the thickness of its weight with its faint smell of musk and heady stimulation. You can't imagine how it constantly provokes such a rousing temptation.

Promise to let me partake of your fruitful essence with its tantric effect. Please forgive me if you think it's somewhat bold to invade your personal space. But these feelings are not to be tamed. You see, these feelings are akin to the wind; they billow, swell, vibrate, and shudder. The rest is better to be shown and forbidden to utter.

Promise to caress me with your eyes and stroke me with your soothing breath. Let your presence engulf me in a blanket of rapture and protection. There's no need for you to search high or low, for I am the elixir to compliment this decadent meal of seduction. We break bread and give a toast as you clasp my hand to lead me through that familiar door to cease any interruption.

I'll only come if you promise that we fall asleep in each other's arms. To nurture the bond forged between us from long ago. We sense the electricity surging through the night air all around us like a cocoon of luminous afterglow.

Promise to make me shout, laugh, and giggle. I love a good joke, a silly face, to keep me breathless with joy. Never mind the toke on a smoke. Turn up the music and watch me churn up a plate of this tantalizing, saucy, wiggle.

Promise to give me an experience that is heartfelt, memorable, and adventurous. Time is on our side now as we count hairs sprinkled with dreaded gray along with a few of those annoying wrinkles. And like the long shadows in the midday sun, we will one day journey into that undeniable fade. Oh, how I will miss your sun-kissed dimples!

I'll only come if you can keep this promise under the moon and stars that coexist within the sacred circle of you and me—yes, we. Echoes of me continuously surround you in spirit. I'm on you here, in you there, everywhere. Tomorrow is never promised, and time is fleeting. There's no time for delay. Take my hand. With purpose, we patiently await the reality of the consented on this much-anticipated day. For this, I come!

Longing

Longing for the chance to hear a seductive whisper. Seeking the unspoken intention of a wink. It's been so long, but I still remember the twirl of that familiar dance.

Longing for the laughter from a tickle. Hoping for a touch as light as a feather. How I cherish the glow of your smile and the depth of those sun-kissed dimples.

Longing for a conversation filled with butterfly emotion, light and airy but deep with color. It thoroughly pleases, like the forbidden fruit, and brings about a zestful elation.

Longing for a moment in the elusive past to turn back the hands of time, a temporary salve to ease the sting of this torment.

Longing for a lasting connection, arms enfolding, tentative holding. For us, there was never a reason for rejection.

Longing for the chase: up, down, here, there, around and around. We surf on cascades of thrills and calm ourselves from the sheer joy of the pace.

Longing for sweet sleep, welcoming your presence in my dreams with no restriction. Wishing for those enchanting nights that I so eagerly seek, relishing their peace.

Longing for the nearness of your spirit—warm, thoughtful, and strong. I'm always open, only for you, my love. My golden dearest, in your arms, I belong.

Longing to gaze upon your face if only for a minute. Your lips, I frantically trace. The thought causes such a swoon and constantly puts me in a state of reflection and daze.

Longing for too long. It's time to fine-tune for the next interlude. Notes played in the key of WE major. Your memory sustains me as our hearts beat in unison to the symphony of the love we create. It's a potent and such an endearing song and for this, I will forever long.

Loveland

You light my fire—soon to be my one desire. You're my love.

I re-create the love we make. I'm not the same. Oh, take my heart.

Come with me. Let's sail away to a place where we cast away our fears, our tears.

It seems to me we both agree; our loyalty to one another is a fact.

My love for you, so true. You're not like any other; that's where it's at.

I'm your wind, so let's fly away to our love-land. Don't be afraid to feel. It's so real.

I'm for you. Whatever you want, I'll do. Love of mine, with you, I'm going to take my time to touch and to trust my love.

You are my joy. You fill me up such a priceless treasure. None compares to you.

You call on me like one, two, three …Don't hesitate. I'm already there.

Can't you see there's no limit to what I'll do for you?

No matter come what may come, I'll cherish you; it's so true.

I'm for you. Whatever you want, I'll do. Love of mine, with you, I'm going to take my time to give and to feel my love.

I love you more than words can say, my love. I won't walk away from you; it takes two.

Come with me to love-land. Glide upon the wind. We're soaring.

Together, we can take a chance. Hand in hand, our love will guide us through. It's so true, my love.

Joy

A Humble Prayer

Thank you, Heavenly Father, for this blessed day. Thank you for waking me up and keeping me safe as I went along the way.

Thank you for watching over my family, friends, and those less fortunate, whether near or far. You are the alpha and omega. You are the morning and night. Your love and mercy are immeasurable. Your skillful hands made the vast universe. You are my supreme master—my redeemer and unfailing star.

I humbly ask that you restore my health and grant me a peaceful sleep. Take away my worries and stress, my aches and pains. I know that all this is possible when I simply call upon your powerful name.

Forgive my trespasses and any ill-will toward others as I learn to obey. Please continue to guide me toward the path to righteousness. For this, Heavenly Father, I humbly pray. Amen.

My Intended, So Sweet

To my intended, so sweet. A love so strong for me.

To my intended, so free. In love, so strong, are we.

On the day that I met you, you looked my way, but it didn't faze me.

You said hello. I turned away. I was shy. Maybe another day.

Calling me, you tried again. You spoke to me with love. I had to let you in.

On the phone until the break of dawn. We talked and talked, and we went on and on.

Thoughts of you, running through my mind. Never thought we would redefine.

I must admit, you're heaven sent. You spoke to me with love and broke down all my self-defense.

It's the sweetest feeling in the world. Your love, I adore and cherish. I'm so glad you're in my life. With you, I'm so blessed to share this.

To my intended, so sweet. A love so strong for me.

To my intended, so free. In love, so strong, are we.

Look at time—how it passed us by. So deep in love, we truly touched the sky.

Through thick and thin, our love would win. My heart's for you, oh darling, until the end.

On the day that I met you, you spoke to me with love. I had to dedicate

my heart to you, such a sweet refrain. So deep in love. I'll never be the same.

My Love Comes

My love comes. My love hums.

I am enchanted by his walk as he unabashedly talks that talk. His essence softly caresses me like satin sheets on a four-poster Queen Anne bed. He playfully teases but often pleases, awakening dormant hopes and dreams planted from so long ago. Who am I to deny the unbridled afterglow?

He comforts me and puts my spirit at ease. He's strong and at times a roguish thug, but always good-natured and so easy to love. It's my privilege to please.

When he gives me that look, I can easily read the signs of the notion. I sit in quiet reflection to visualize the scene. At times, it comes to me in black and white, more frequently in color, but always in slow motion.

My love comes. My love hums.

He's always one to uplift and brighten my day. I must admit without hesitation, he's such a precious gift in every imaginable way. In my heart, may he never part. He will forever stay. Waking up in his arms is not only a precious gift but a true addiction. Strong arms cradling me; warm bodies surrounded in a cascade of fragrant waterfalls and spices of love. I, the jury, reach a unanimous decision.

Often when we are together, there's no need for heavy discussion. We coexist in mutual contemplation. His meekness alone provokes such unrelenting temptation. We speak through silent emotion: a smile, the lover's gaze, and sometimes the slightest touch. It's written in the resounding vibration. Yes, we get off on this kind of seductive rush.

My love comes. My love hums.

We set a slow pace as we hold and mold our bodies together. Face-to-face is what we seek. Sweeter than sweet, deeper than deep, round and round in a consensual synchronicity, we strive to reach that ultimate peak.

Who are we to deny the raging fire as we lift each other higher and higher to consume the swirling tendrils of our desire? We no longer have use for standard words of English. We express ourselves in a secret language, called WE. The familiar words, "Oh baby," are transformed into a symphony of sounds: "Ah-a-bee, ah-a-bee."

The repeated phrase, "Give it to me," becomes rearranged in a tangible echo of whispers: "Goo-ta-meh!", Goo-ta-meh!"

Yes, we are on that level indeed—quenching our thirst, unselfishly giving and receiving, fulfilling that need. As we float onto a cloud of brief interlude, we shift gears to ease up on the pedal, catch a shaky breath, and feebly attempt to breathe. It's all about that trust, and for this, we truly believe. There's no denying, so stop even trying. For this kind of love, I'm most certainly buying! And as the dawn rises in the distance, once again, we heave. We go hard, fully charged, taking it all as we scream each other's name! He gives. I take. We receive.

My love comes. My love hums.

I am enchanted by this walk (moans) as he unabashedly talks that talk (feathery kisses). His essence softly caresses me like satin sheets on a four-poster Queen Anne bed (holding). He playfully teases but often pleases, awakening dormant hopes and dreams planted from so long ago. Who am I to deny this, the remarkable afterglow? Never let go; never letting go.

Mee clo wa. (I love you.) Clo tae woo. (Love is you.)

Solitude Groove

In my solitude, I sometimes shake and shudder with fear, wondering and pondering about the unknowns in this life that may be drawing near. Maybe it's just my colorful imagination or an overdosed anxiety that causes this hesitation.

I sometimes talk to myself or to her, him and them. We cry, laugh, and holler. At times, I'm asked, "What was that?" I simply adjust my glasses and say, "Oh, nothing. Never mind. Don't bother."

I sometimes contemplate on the could've and would've, praying that it's not too late. It took me a while to make it all come together, and now, I'm surely sliding into home plate.

I say a pray for the earth, children, animals, and families, wishing all are healthy, safe, and protected by THEE. I realize that nothing remains the same. Each season brings a new rhyme, a transcendental reason. It's inevitable: we change.

I meditate to rejuvenate the life force beating inside of me. I nurture it, encourage it and fill it with healing light to keep me sound and sure throughout the bustling day and the starlit night.

In my solitude, I make notes and plan for my day, paying close attention to details before I pack and be on my way. I continue to coexist and enjoy life in a harmonious mood, trying not to disturb this serene solitude groove.

No Lie

I'm not going to lie. For a love lost, I cried. It changed me, rearranged me, and took me for a swoop. I tumbled and turned. I thought and I fought. I got caught up in an intoxicating romantic loop. Oh, how I looked forward to the next adventure. Every touch and laugh, I've held close and will always remember.

It's funny how we blow on the dice and take a chance on romance. The forbidden fruit always seems the sweetest. It excites and warms the blood with mindless passion and tempts us like no other. We try to sustain, fight to abstain. We failed the class on etiquette and meekness.

Love is vacuous, not meant to be contained. It is the blood of life. It is even the life we breathe. It motivates and creates, flows like water in, out, over, and through, often difficult to maintain.

But if I could, I most certainly would, turn back the hands of time, when you were mine, to once again experience our love's sweetest refrain. No lie.

'Ode To My Great-Grandmother

It's a modest Monday. I can still remember the smell of the lima beans cooking in her old cast-iron pot. I set the table. We pray and begin to eat. We talk about our plans for the upcoming week: attending piano lessons and going into town to shop.

On Tuesday, we rise early for breakfast. Afterwards, I skip to the shed to get stacks and racks before we trek to the garden. We chop weeds and pick fruit and vegetables that would bring a good bargain.

Every Wednesday, we eat a meal of Monday's leftovers. She takes out the ledger to pay the bills. I begin to wash the dishes as she puts food away. We laugh heartily as she tells a childhood story. Wow! It was such a thrill.

On Thursday, we travel to town to pick up supplies, and then we're homeward bound. We make a quick stop to check on friends and family but no more dallying around.

Friday evening, in the air is the aroma of fried catfish to go with the vegetables we picked. The sun slowly sets through the old windowpane, and all is quiet with newspaper read. "Night-night, Mama's baby child," she says as she slowly bends on ancient knees to pray and kiss my youthful head.

Saturday morning brings a day of cleaning and toting clothes through the back porch to hang on the clothesline. It's a warm and breezy day, with the scent of magnolia blossoms lingering in the July air as she hums a favorite hymn and hands me the clothes basket, but I don't mind.

Sunday, the Lord's Day in every way. The house is filled with calm—no work or play. The table overflows with a Sunday dinner of chicken and dressing, sweet potatoes, fresh greens, and such. But that was long ago, when I was a mere child. Yes, I've been blessed. I was touched.

But it's not quite the same as I come out of my revelry, pause, and catch a shaky breath to hum one of her favorite hymns, "Nearer My God to Thee." She was a warm soul, and filled with an overflowing wealth. The memories are precious, and I will hold them forever in a special place deep within my chest. She did a job well done, nurtured her offspring, and was often put to the test. In the ninety-eight years of her life, she was a survivor and remained steadfast and for this, she was granted a much-needed heavenly rest.

But there are times when I become doubtful and somewhat weak, for this life is unrelenting and creates such a downpour of unsteady beats. Because I'm still wishing, still missing, and forever kissing my great-grandmother so much.

In memory of my great-grandmother Dee as experienced through my life as a child. Forever missing you.

A Ray Of Golden Light

Almost broken; tired and worn out, often cautious and indecisive—not

knowing where to turn, and full of doubt. Trying to stay up and trying to find my way.

Thirsty for a cup of reassurance, a salve of compassion, or a ray of golden light. For these, I would certainly pay.

Falling and tumbling. Tumbling and falling. It becomes harder to thrive and takes a toss of a coin to even survive.

Up, down, merry-go-round and round-go-merry. Steadily tripping and constantly bending.

I shout! "Save me!" "Deliver me!" Redeem me!" "Forgive me!" "Please, Lord, make me over!"

As I sit within the black pit of myself, steadily drowning and choking on this unforgiving misery. An anchoring voice somewhere in the distance, strong and steady, says, "Reach out and grab my hand." I take a firm grip, find my footing, catch a shaky breath, and begin this rebirth: a new journey. My new quest.

Steadily climbing and climbing steady. Up, up, and farther up, learning better to shield myself from the falling rocks of life that come my way. Doing my best to wipe away the sands of bitterness and resentment that blanket my tear stained eyes. "It's going to get better," I tell myself. If I can only keep my eyes on the prize. There's just twenty-four hours in a day. As mama would say, "Tomorrow is a gift." With one last resounding shout, I purge myself of the shackles of negativity, swim through the sea of insecurity and leave behind the remainder of that overflowing drift.

A doctor once said, "Take a deep breath, bear down, and give one last push." So I pushed: ten, nine, eight, and something snaps. I see a flicker of that reassuring light. I feel a tear and a strong pull from deep within. Now, wait a minute. Let me reposition myself to further comprehend. And oh, how I push: seven, six, five! Let me slow down a minute to bring up my knees so that I can see what lies beyond those trees. There, right there! I finally see the prize in the distance—the new pathway of living and being. The lit road to a better me: four, three, two, one …I won!

Was almost broken but not ruined. Was tired and worn out. But, now rejuvenated, optimistic, and full of hope, forget about any doubt. I'm on my way up and out! Tried herbs, medicines, therapists, and such. But now, I try God, who redeems me, He sustains me, and He forgives me! Oh, how I love Him!

I give it all to God, who stretched out his hand to lift me and show me the right footing. Who protected and shielded me from the raging storms. For He is the ray of golden light that saved me, and now I am whole, made over in light—yes, reborn! Amen!

See Me

Do you see me?

I want you to, so stop trying to avoid the inevitable, and just be honest; stay true.

Do you feel me?

I know that you do. Watch me in motion here, there, and everywhere; observe my essence, humility, and devotion.

Do you hear me?

I need you to. Appreciate my respect and commitment for you. No more misunderstandings, setbacks, or resentments.

Do you see me?

I feel that you do. I don't care about fame or critical opinions. You are in my heart. We are forever connected. Whether right or wrong, no one is perfect, and all is forgiven.

Sister To Sister

My sister is my number-one fan. She has mother's delicate nose, freckles, and industrious hands. When I lose my way and need encouragement, I hear her motherly voice, and I am revived. My cup is soon filled within.

She's the natural organizer. Everything around her is neat and clean. She's known as the sweet one, the meek one, and is sometimes timid, shy, or hurried. But when I see her now, confident and self-assured, I'm no longer worried.

My sister's life almost ended, with high temperatures, terrible aches, and such. Man, she gave us such a fright. She could barely eat or sleep. The doctor shook his head; he was put to an amazing test. We took her home and prayed day and night and put our faith in the Lord to do what was best.

My sister is wise—a kind spirit and a nurturing mother. She's well, full of cheer, and blessed like no other. I couldn't imagine my life without her. She is strong and resilient, never one to give up a fight. My Redeemer lives and joy comes in the morning, because I knew that with God in charge, everything would turn out just right.

Thank you, Lord!

Sitting Here

Sitting here, wishing you were near.

Longing and yearning for you, my dear…..here

To be close to me, see me, and touch me. Those cherished memories are forever ingrained in our hearts and minds; in this life, we will forever be

I'm sitting here still caught up in the never ending rapture of WE. I must admit and without hesitation, I adore our times together, you and me.

Sitting here, restless. Breathless in this complex position. But the feelings run deep as I attempt to adjust and show a good face through this ripple of transition.

Sitting here, haunted by the shadows, whispers, and scents: the remnants of our existence in the elusive past.

I try. I cry. I talk. I walk. But in reality, I know our time has forever passed.

Sitting here, contemplating, anxious and ready for the day to just be in your space. All you have to do is give a sigh and a simple hi, and I'm there—no matter the time or place.

Sitting here, trying to keep things together and get my head right, but I may as well stop fooling myself. I welcome the peace of sleep. You constantly visit my dreams during the busy day and endless nights.

Sitting here, trying to calm my spirit within, but it's a struggle. Sometimes I relent to take a break, and just give in.

I give in to the essence of you. Oh, the flower petal memories of you. The breath of you. Oh, how I miss you so—the colors of you. Oh, my love, you can't imagine or even know. I'm forever longing for just one more youthful, carefree rendezvous. Man the ship, hoist the sails, and away we go.

Sitting here, trying to cope. Feeling sweaty and thick as If I'm on some funky dope—so high with you. I believe I can touch the jazzy-blue sky. My, my, my, how we did fly.

I know I need to stop this show, put a period, move forward, and turn the page. It's better to let time heal and just let it go.

Sitting here missing, wishing, and forever kissing. You can't count the measure or define the distance. And to the extent, I guess you'll never know. So here, I sit.

Time To Make A Change

Is it right for me to hide it?

I've had enough; no longer fighting.

I'm strong enough this time to let you go.

This heart of mine can't take it anymore.

No looking back; I'm walking out that door.

I've had enough now—time to change.

Got to move on and rearrange.

My life with you—so sad; it's true. I've got to let go.

And I can't stop loving you.

And I want to say we're through.

And I can't—and I don't—want to let you go.

Time for you to make a change.

No more excuses, and don't complain.

Your life with me—so sad to see; how could this be?

And I just can't hide it. Oh, no, I just can't.

The kids are older and away at college.

We've had some good times, I'll acknowledge.

I've given you the best years of my life.

We gave and took to make it all come right.

But I'll be on my way, come morning light.

I've had enough now—said I'm through.

Got to move on, stop loving you.

Why can't you see? Darling, please:

I've got to save me.

I've had enough now—time to change.

Got to move on and rearrange.

My life with you: so sad; it's true. I've got to let go.

And I can't stop loving you.

And I want to say we're through.

And I can't—and I don't—want to let you go.

Time for you to make a change.

No more excuses, and don't complain.

Your life with me—so sad to see; how could this be?

And I just can't hide it.

Transform

Time to perform to the best of your ability. One and two, do you, and I'll remain me unequivocally. Rise for the prize set before your eyes. It's a struggle, but you can make it double.

With knowledge and strong will, say no to foolish thrills and stay focused mentally. Don't get caught up in the notion, stay on point and be ready for the task. Stay sharp and flow steady to persevere and achieve your goal at last.

People may talk with criticism, shun your ways, and say you're to blame. But what's destined for you will be just for you, with no one else's name.

Sometimes, sacrifice is the price to pay to reach the peak of success, so save the champagne for later. The journey may put you to the test, but don't digress; realize that you've been favored. But remember to stay humble and be respectful, even to the haters.

Patience and kindness are sometimes few, but they're essential to accomplish this attainable dream. Hold loved ones dear, and keep good friends close and a few of those point guards will certainly come in handy for your team.

Time to perform. Your tools are polished and ready, but be cautious, not thoughtless, as you start out on the track. Pay attention to the highways and byways to determine your steps with surety, purpose, and tact.

It's sometimes inevitable to stray from the norm, to be reborn. But live your life for you and try to create an upstanding way. But don't forget, it's necessary to repent and bow on bended knees to be thankful for waking with the sun each and every day.

There's a knocking upon your door. The world is yours to explore, and may the Lord shield you from life's turbulent storms. Be a keeper of peace, and have compassion for those less fortunate who are sometimes weak.

You can never go wrong by performing a good deed. What you put in is what you get back, and for this, you must believe. And just like family, the sting of your own blade may cut you deep, but we don't cast them away, there is still use and purpose, we still cherish; we keep.

The bells are chiming to announce your timing. It's a contraction of passion, an undulating surge of release to be transformed!

The bells are chiming to announce your timing. It's a contraction of passion, an undulating surge of release to be......TRANSFORMED!

The bells are chiming to announce your timing. It's a contraction of passion, an undulating surge of release to be......TRANSFORMED!

Trying To Find My Way

Sitting here, reminiscing, wishing, thinking, and just trying to find my way.

The other day, I was optimistic, ritualistic, and on point. Not waiting for the man; had my own master plan. Funny how things can change so quickly; that was only yesterday.

It's the never-ending struggle of balancing and facing those challenges head on. Organize this to manage that, and make some jolly attempt to live in the so-called parallel of righteousness.

After all, the kids are watching, learning, and needing. Forget the negotiating and pleading; no questioning the question. Do what you have to do. Time waits for no one, so embrace your struggle, as a friend once said. Don't give up the fight!

Sitting here, feeling disenchanted. Received the unexpected news that a loved one was ill. It brought on such a wave of distress. I ran from here to there, pushed to the limit, all in a panic. I was definitely put to the test, but through God's grace, I eventually managed.

Interesting how one can be so motivated to be true, brand new, hopeful, and determined within. But like the unpredictable shift and slide of life, we sometimes falter and become altered, get turned around, and miss that pole in the hole, trying to make up for past sins.

I sit here, but I'm not really here. I'm actually over there, over yonder, in my mind and spirit. But this body is trained to perform like clockwork though, and I go through all the textbook motions: do, did, done, and then next.

I bend and blend. I blink and think. I pick up to put down. Give this; they take that. Oh, it has to get done and with attention to detail. But sometimes with no enthusiasm. I simply go through the paces, robotically, with no sentiment or emotion.

But it's not for me to complain. I'm just trying to maintain with commitment, strength, and determination. It's a part of that essence of life, the struggle, joys, and strife. But I try to hold on, if only with a thread of optimism to sew a measure of some hope even still.

The equation is: 2b over self-preservation, multiplied by me, to equal the sum that is us. It's no periwinkle or fuchsia over here. It's yes or no, do or done. The basic colors of get-it-done green and before-dinnertime blue. See, it's really that simple and altogether true.

But through it all, I'm still here, trying to stay motivated, sweeping away the cobwebs and clearing the fog. It's going to get better, as mama would say. It's all in the attitude. What do you have to lose with prayer and conviction each day? I'm not perfect, and I'm not trying to bump my head again and fall, naw! But who am I fooling? I can't do it all. So, I'm going to give it to the Lord to strengthen me, to help me find a new beginning from this ending—to find my way.

You Only Had To Say

What is it?

You only had to say that you missed me, you're glad to see me, or dreamed of kissing me—just waiting for the day. You only had to show that you understood and wished that we could. Yes, the feeling was mutual. I was already there. But, didn't you know?

You only had to be a friend in need, no selfishness, and no greed, just simple. You didn't have to put on fancy airs for me. You only had to keep it real that you couldn't wait—no reason to hesitate. The truth, I can always take, because I'm a big girl now. I know the deal.

You only had to stop and listen to my tone, my anxious moan. These were the signs of my true admission. You only had to take the time to be a part. But we failed to start—too late to be mine. You only had to give a little of yourself. Why put us on a dusty shelf? Happiness is essential; it's time to live.

You only had to open your eyes to see: no longer the child running wild, but a woman strong in her essence. Yes, it's me.

What is it?

You only had to be aware of the subtle emotions; no games, no potions—just the core of me, a friend who genuinely cared. You only had to be understanding. I know your life is demanding, but I'm flexible. I can only ask; no commanding. You only had to give a little consideration, change position, walk around in my shoes to gain of sense of how I live—to truly understand the situation. You only had to say … but the hour grows short, time is fleeting, and we're forever pleading for just one more day.

You Put The Color Back In My Life

You put the color back in my life.

Your light saved me. It took me from a bleak state of existence and rescued me from a world of despair. You gave me a reason for believing, for seeing that someone on earth took the time and still cared.

You gave me a reason to rise, and because of this, I now thrive. The love flowed, and I became whole. Like raindrops on a desert rose, I blossomed and survived.

You put the color back in my life.

Your protection and warmth shielded me just enough, for this life can be tumultuous, tedious, and often times rough. But I regained my footing and found a new path, a better way. And for this, I was able to refocus, find my bearings. No longer lost and running astray. With a soft touch, kind words, and a look that would make any girl blush, my, my, my, you gave me such a rush. But life is fleeting, and sheer joy I seek. Yes, your queen is speaking to you, my cherished crush. I began to live and breathe again in colors of gracious green, fiery fuchsia, and radiant red. You opened up your heart and gave me a safe haven to calm my nerves and rest an oh-so-weary head.

You put the color back in my life.

I was revived. My body and spirit once again began to glow. But this, I'm sure you already know. Our paths crossed just in the nick of time, and for this experience, I don't regret and will never forget. But why does finding sweet love have to be such a crime?

You put the color back in my life.

And now, I have regained my sight, complete and grateful, yoked with the colors of hope, love, beauty, respect, and adoration------your essence, your precious light.

My gratitude, I give to you.

What If I Flipped On You?

What if I flipped on you, huh?

What if I took a view, huh?

Would you love me for you?

Would you always be true?

No more excuses and no more complaints.

I'm breaking loose and taking off these chains.

I'm going to stand up for myself now.

I want to be footloose and fancy-free.

I'm tired of talking, and it's time for you to see:

I'm taking that loop back to "Interstate Me."

These are critical times; no more lying.

Take no chances; I'm through with trying.

You can't shake me, no, no.

You can't break me, No!

I'm turning this whole thing around and moving forward to be found.

No more talking; it's time for walking

on the track, no turning back. I'm moving forward, so step back.

No more extensions. You've used up all your minutes.

No more deadlines or final good-bye kisses.

Time to pull up, go hit it and quit it.

One, two, three, time to do me.

I told you once; I told you twice:

You should've taken your BFF's advice.

You can't hold me back no more, so get your stroll on; walk out the door.

You can't break me, no, no.

You can't shake me, No!

I'm going to turn this whole thing around, move forward—touch down!

Stay well and cherished!

Printed in the United States
By Bookmasters